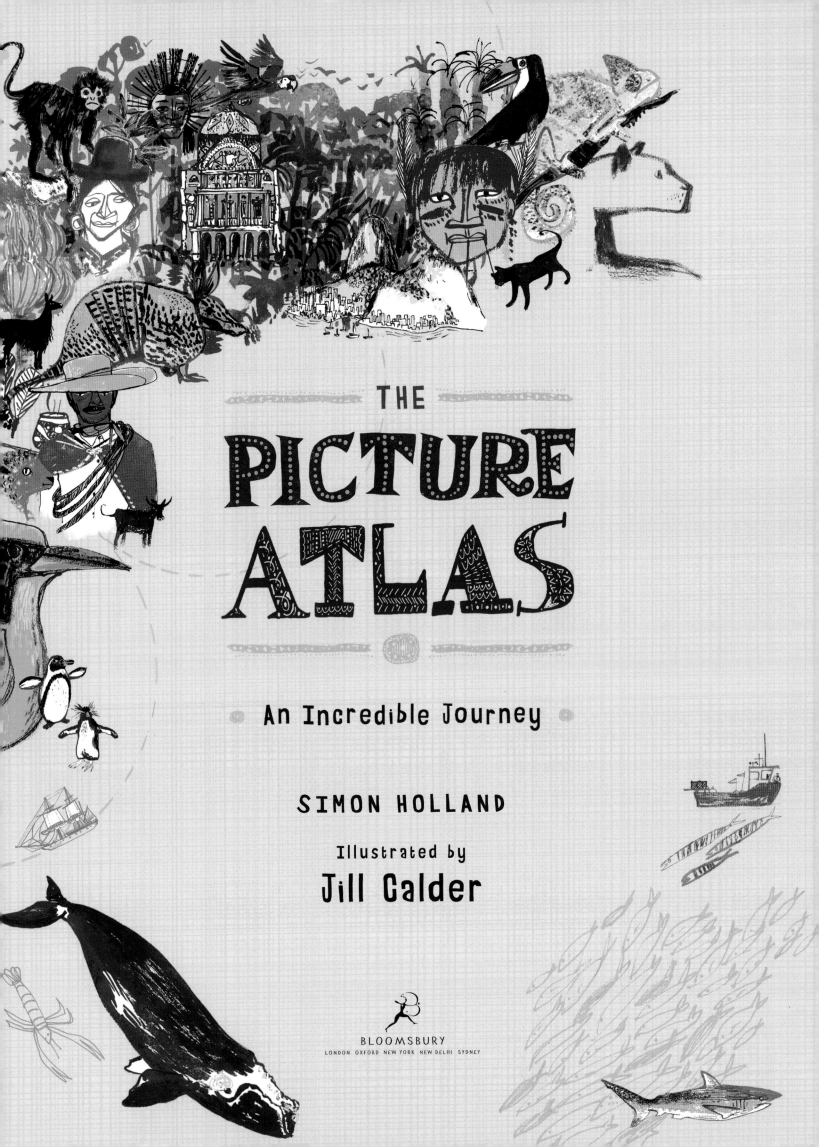

THE
PICTURE
ATLAS

An Incredible Journey

SIMON HOLLAND

Illustrated by
Jill Calder

BLOOMSBURY
LONDON OXFORD NEW YORK NEW DELHI SYDNEY

Bloomsbury Children's Books
An imprint of Bloomsbury Publishing Plc

50 Bedford Square, London WC1B 3DP UK

www.bloomsbury.com

BLOOMSBURY and the Diana logo are trademarks of Bloomsbury Publishing Plc

First published in Great Britain 2017

ISBN 978 1 4088 8486 7

2 4 6 8 10 9 7 5 3 1

Printed and bound in Italy by L.E.G.O. S.p.A. Vicenza, Italy

MIX
Paper from
responsible sources
FSC® C023419

To find out more about our authors and books visit www.bloomsbury.com. Here you will find extracts,
author interviews, details of forthcoming events and the option to sign up for our newsletters.

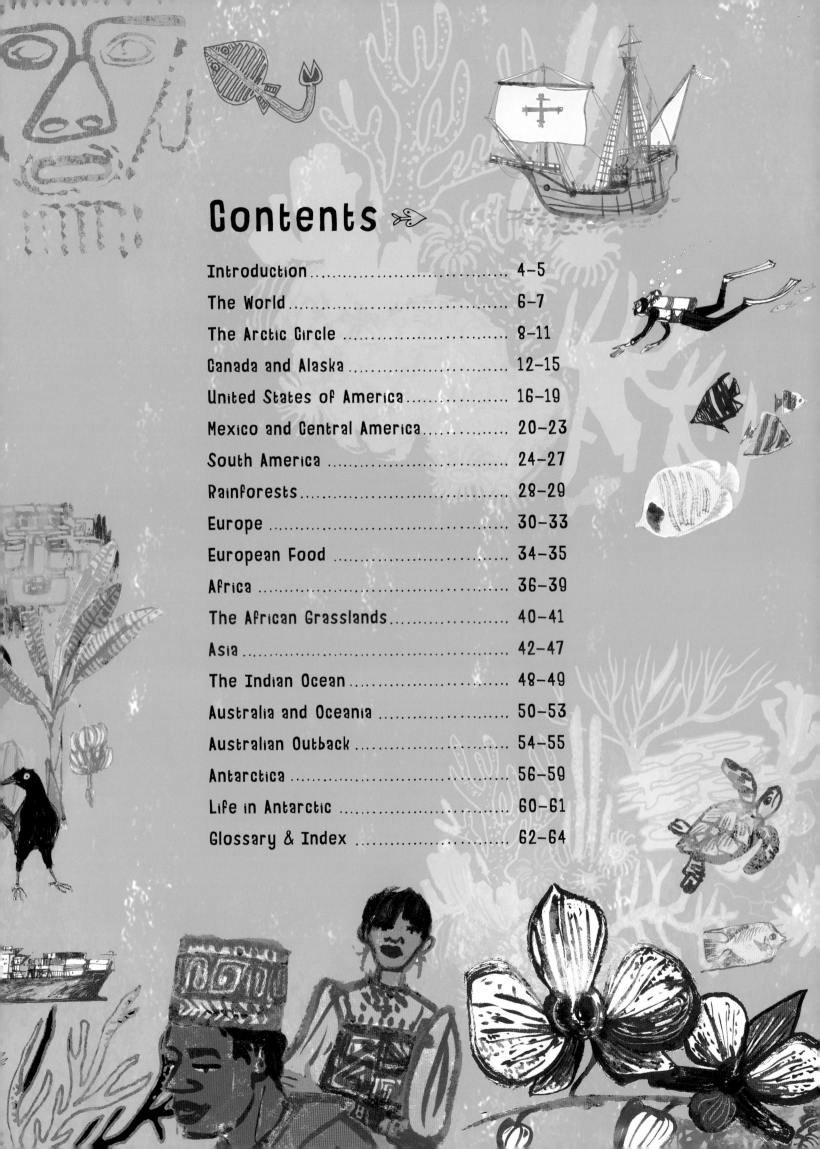

Contents

Introduction

The Earth is just one of billions of planets across the universe, but it's a truly special one. It sits in a comfortable, cosy orbit around a blazing star - the Sun - at just the right distance for lots of incredible things to come to life. The temperatures are just right for water to swirl around the surface of the planet (in massive amounts), and the atmosphere is thick enough to protect living things and stop the water from steaming up into space. Lots of water means an incredible amount of amazing and fascinating life forms can exist all around the globe.

Over billions of years (around 4.54 billion years to be precise) the crusty 'plates' making up the Earth's surface have drifted very slowly – on top of hot, gooey rocks – into seven continents, splitting the world into lots of different zones. Each one has a unique blend of plants, animals, and people, as well as a different climate. This has made the world extraordinarily diverse, dynamic, and dramatic!

The gradual chopping-up into continents has also turned the Earth's gigantic ocean into lots of different water worlds – from shallow, tropical reefs to polar seas and deep, dark trenches several kilometres below the waves. Salty seas cover almost three-quarters of the surface – but once you step onto land, you'll be able to scale mountains, cross deserts, ride rivers, forage in forests, set your sights on cities and then plant your flag at the North and South poles.

So what are you waiting for? Turn the page and let your world wide adventure begin.

NORTH
PACIFIC
OCEAN

NORTH AMERICA

NORTH
ATLANTIC
OCEAN

CENTRAL AMERICA

SOUTH
PACIFIC
OCEAN

SOUTH
AMERICA

SOUTH
ATLANTIC
OCEAN

The WORLD

ARCTIC OCEAN

EUROPE

ASIA

MIDDLE EAST

AFRICA

Tropic of Cancer 23.5° N

Equator 0°

INDIAN
OCEAN

Tropic of Capricorn 23.5° S

AUSTRALIA

OCEANIA

SOUTHERN
OCEAN

h Pole

ANTARCTICA

The ARCTIC CIRCLE

NORTH PACIFIC OCEAN

Orca

Arctic poppy

Aurora Borealis
(Northern Lights)

Musk ox

CANADA

QUEE
ELIZAB
ISLAN

Snow goose

HUDSON
BAY

BA
B

BAFFIN
ISLAND

The Inuit

DAVIS STRAIT

Nuuk

Bearberry

NORTH ATLAN

Atlantic cod

The
ARCTIC
CIRCLE

· ·

The top and bottom bits of the Earth are where the planet gets very chilly. Don't come to the Arctic expecting to wear those new shorts - the temperatures can get as low as -50°C (or even lower, brrrr).

The Arctic Circle is a mini-world of snow-white water. The North Pole doesn't sit on land, but is adrift in the middle of an ocean that freezes over for most of the year. All of the freezing Arctic seas are encircled by ice-cold, northern lands. The southern fringes of these lands are trimmed by the tundra regions, which are cold and dry.

Skating around the Arctic Circle, you'll find lots of different people who live amongst the ice and snow - fishing, hunting and getting all they need from the natural resources around them. Take a tour around the Circle and meet the Sami (or Lapps) of northern Europe, the Nenets and the Yakut people of Siberia, or the Chukchi of northeastern Asia.

THE INUIT →

The Inuit have survived on a diet of raw meat and fish for thousands of years. It's a very fatty diet and gives them the nourishment they need. This is why they were once known as Eskimos - a name that comes from a native word meaning 'eater of raw meat'. The name Inuit simply means 'the people'.

The Inuit are descended from migrating people who have lived in northern parts of Alaska (U.S.A), Canada, Greenland and Siberia (Russia) for many thousands of years.

Snow geese return to the tundra regions in the Arctic summer. When hundreds of them fly together, it's called a 'snowstorm'!

TUNDRA

The tundra regions, towards the south of the Arctic region, have lots of plant and animal life. There the landscape is frozen all or nearly all year round. In spring, the tundra is covered with colour, as plants quickly flower and produce seeds. Hundreds of migrating birds flock to the tundra and animals such as musk oxen, reindeer and the Arctic fox have their babies.

The skin of a polar bear is actually . . . black!

Alaskan bear

ARCTIC OCEAN

BEAUFORT SEA

Brown bear

ALASKA (USA)

Alaskan salmon

Great Bear Lake

NORTHWEST TERRITO...

Wolf

Oil pipeline

HOTEL

Salmon drying

YUKON TERRITORY

Pasqueflower

Caribou

● ANCHORAGE

19th-century gold prospector

King crab

GULF OF ALASKA

Albertosaurus

Orca

BRITISH COLUMBIA

NORTH PACIFIC OCEAN

Totem pole

Vancouver ●

CANADA AND ALASKA

Mountie (Canadian police woman)

Inuit owl art

Minke whale

Orca fins

BAFFIN BAY

Inuit fisherman

Inuit fish hook

DAVIS STRAIT

Inuit fish traps

NUNAVUT

CANADA

Elk

NORTHWESTERN PASSAGES

HUDSON STRAIT

Henry Hudson
EXPLORER
1565–1611

Wolverine

Canadian lynx

HUDSON

BAY

QUÉBEC

LABRADOR SEA

Maple syrup

NEWFOUNDLAND & LABRADOR

Cloudberry

SASKATCHEWAN

MANITOBA

Beaver

Maple leaf

ONTARIO

CN Tower

PRINCE EDWARD ISLAND

Quebec City

NEW BRUNSWICK

Parliament Hill

NOVA SCOTIA

OTTAWA

Montreal

Toronto

USA

Niagara Falls

13

CANADA AND ALASKA

Canada is a country where nature rules supreme. Much of its magnificent scenery is locked up in ice for most of the year, while more than half of it is blanketed by the big, green, boreal forests (which lie south of the Arctic bits). The northern winters are long, dark and cold (plummeting to -40°C in places), which is why most Canadians set up home in the south.

Canada is the second largest nation (a runner-up to Russia): like maple syrup, it spreads out across more than half of North America's big continent. However, only 35 million people live there. That may sound like a crowd but the USA has more than nine times that! It's a place of different voices, too - English and French are the main languages, while a fifth of the people speak other tongues.

Alaska leans out to the west. Although it sits next to Canada it is actually part of the USA, who bought the land from Russia, way back in 1867. Alaska is a valuable, oil-rich place, where gold is also found, and it's home to the ten tallest mountains in the USA. Watch out for the incredible wildlife - brown bears fish for salmon as they launch themselves upstream.

PREHISTORIC CANADA

Alberta, home of the Dinosaur Provincial Park, is one of the world's richest dinosaur fossil sites. Seventy-five million years ago its landscape was a subtropical paradise overflowing with giant redwood trees, palms, giant ferns, and dinosaurs. Forty dinosaur species have been discovered in the park. Albertosaurus and Edmontosaurus are just two of these, and are named after places in Canada.

Europeans began sailing to Canada in the 16th and 17th centuries, and many of them were French. They explored the Great Lakes, looking for places where fur trappers could hunt for animal skins.

Totem poles are made by traditional artists from the northwest coast of North America. The animal characters on the totem pole have special meaning in the local culture.

Niagara Falls is an awesome set of waterfalls spanning the border between Canada and the USA. The three waterfalls are Horseshoe Falls, American Falls and Bridal Veil Falls. An average of 2,400 cubic metres of water rushes over the falls every second.

Cherries

WASHINGTON

ZN ZN ZN ZN
ZN ZN ZN
ZN ZN ZN

30 ZN ZINC

Zinc mining

Buffalo

MONTANA

Logging

Wolf

Prairie
dog

NORTH DAKOTA

IDAHO

Prairie schooner

SOUTH DAKOTA

Mining truck

WYOMING

Torna

Giant Redwoods

Golden Gate Bridge

Vineyards

OREGON

Combine
harvester

Mount Rushmore

NEVADA

NEBRASKA

San Francisco

Silicon Valley

Saguaro
cacti

DEATH
VALLEY

Death Valley

UTAH

COLORADO

Ammonite
fossil

Petroglyph figure

Navajo
woman

KAN

CALIFORNIA

ROUTE
66

Monument Valley

Los Angeles

ARIZONA

Joshua tree

NEW MEXICO

Kokopelli
(Hopi symbol)

OKLAHOM

Long

Navajo magpie

PACIFIC OCEAN

BAJA CALIFORNIA

GULF OF CALIFORNIA

Hopi woman

Desert tortoise

Oil pump

Ranch

MEXICO

TEXA

Blue whales

UNITED STATES ★ OF ★ AMERICA

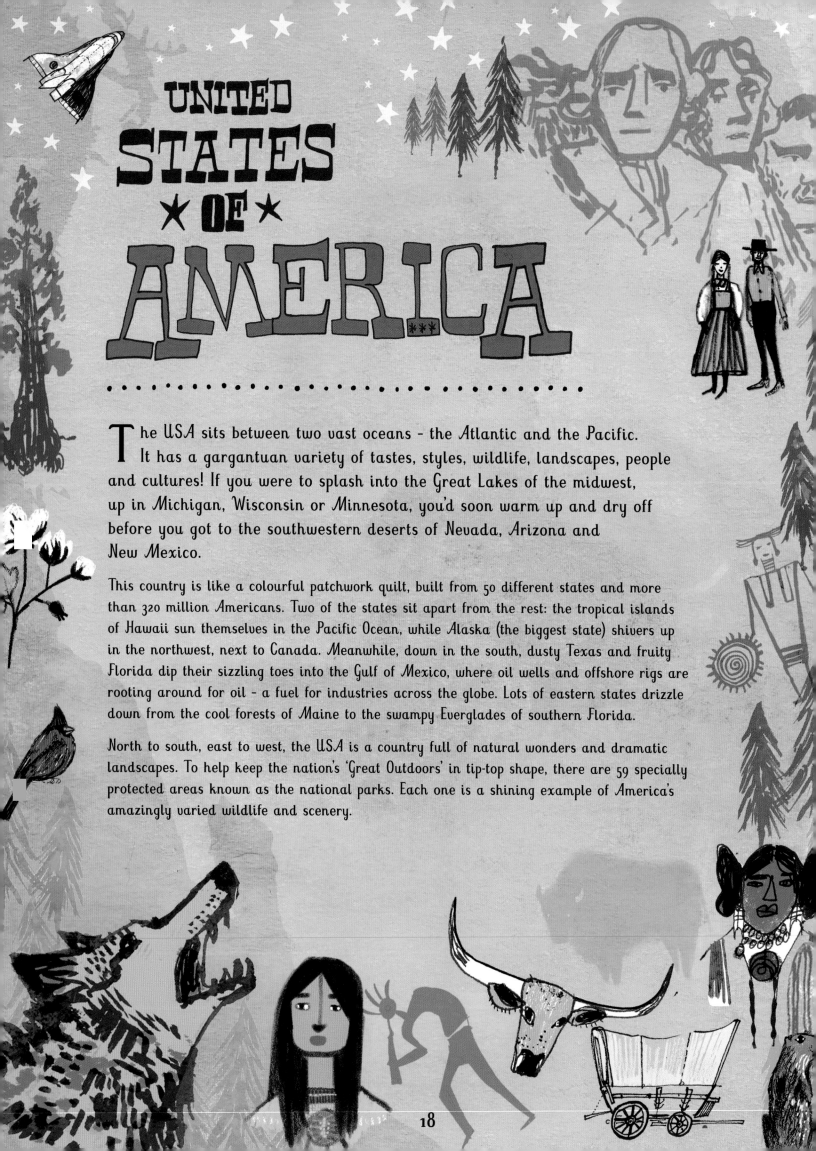

The USA sits between two vast oceans – the Atlantic and the Pacific. It has a gargantuan variety of tastes, styles, wildlife, landscapes, people and cultures! If you were to splash into the Great Lakes of the midwest, up in Michigan, Wisconsin or Minnesota, you'd soon warm up and dry off before you got to the southwestern deserts of Nevada, Arizona and New Mexico.

This country is like a colourful patchwork quilt, built from 50 different states and more than 320 million Americans. Two of the states sit apart from the rest: the tropical islands of Hawaii sun themselves in the Pacific Ocean, while Alaska (the biggest state) shivers up in the northwest, next to Canada. Meanwhile, down in the south, dusty Texas and fruity Florida dip their sizzling toes into the Gulf of Mexico, where oil wells and offshore rigs are rooting around for oil – a fuel for industries across the globe. Lots of eastern states drizzle down from the cool forests of Maine to the swampy Everglades of southern Florida.

North to south, east to west, the USA is a country full of natural wonders and dramatic landscapes. To help keep the nation's 'Great Outdoors' in tip-top shape, there are 59 specially protected areas known as the national parks. Each one is a shining example of America's amazingly varied wildlife and scenery.

The bald eagle is the USA's famous national bird. In the 1960s just a few hundred were left, but today you can spot this handsome and fearsome predator near large bodies of water all over the USA.

· ·

EXPLORE THE EAST

The Appalachian Mountains prop up the northeastern states of the USA, where rabbits, rodents, woodpeckers, owls, foxes, squirrels, hares and bears all thrive in their cool forest habitats. The southeastern corner of the country couldn't be more different. The Everglades of Florida form a huge expanse of boggy land, mostly underwater, covered by tall grasses. It's a perfect place for tall, wading birds and aquatic (water-based) reptiles such as turtles, alligators, snakes and lizards.

Dipping into the sea, from north to south, you can keep your eyes peeled for humpback whales, grey whales, eared seals, northern elephant seals, sea otters and, of course, those playful California sea lions.

· · — · · — · · — · · — · · — · · — · · — ·

IT'S A TWISTER!!

The vast, flat expanses of the Great Plains, in the heart of the USA, are the playground of tornadoes. Chilly winds from Canada and the Rocky Mountains skip down and meet up with the warm, damp air that comes from the Gulf of Mexico – the perfect ingredients for a twister with the power to suck a well dry or heave herds of cattle into a violent sky.

· · · · · · · · · · · · · · · · · · ·

Modern miner

Gila monster

Old silver mine

USA

MEXICO

19th-century silver miner

Jackup rig

GULF OF MEXICO

Elephant seal

Mayan wolf sculpture

Mexico City Cathedral

Chichén Itzá

Tol... fig...

Hernán Cortés

● MEXICO CITY

Volcano Popocatépetl

Grey whale

BEL...

BELIZ...

Tikal

GUATEMALA

GUATEMALA CITY ●

HON... TEGUC...

PACIFIC OCEAN

Day of the Dead skull

Howler monkey

SAN SALVADOR ●
EL SALVADOR

MANA...

Eagle ray

Cac... po...

MEXICO CENTRAL & AMERICA

Tulum face

Shark

ATLANTIC OCEAN

Christopher Columbus

Santa Maria

Green turtle

NASSAU

THE BAHAMAS

HAVANA

CUBA

Sugar cane

Sugar cane worker

Coffee beans

Avocado

Diego Velázquez de Cuéllar

CAYMAN ISLANDS

HAITI

BRITISH VIRGIN ISLANDS

PUERTO RICO

JAMAICA • KINGSTON

DOMINICAN REPUBLIC

ANGUILLA

US VIRGIN ISLANDS

ST KITTS & NEVIS

ANTIGUA & BARBUDA

CARIBBEAN SEA

MONTSERRAT

GUADELOUPE

DOMINICA

Banana tree

Kuna symbol

MARTINIQUE

Urraca bird

Kuna woman

ST LUCIA

ARUBA

ST VINCENT & THE GRENADINES

OSÉ

STA CA

CURAÇAO

BARBADOS

Orchids

GRENADA

Panama canal

PANAMA CITY

PANAMA

TRINIDAD & TOBAGO

Container ship

SOUTH AMERICA

MEXICO & CENTRAL & AMERICA

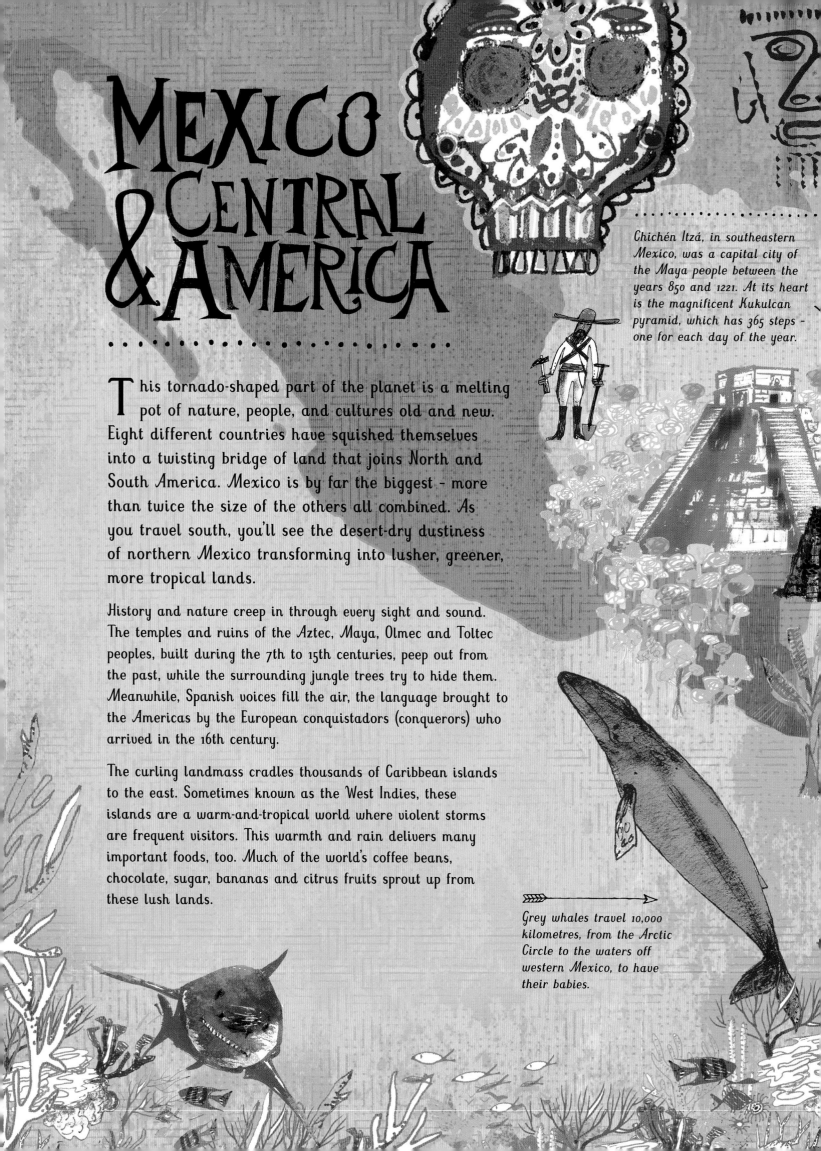

Chichén Itzá, in southeastern Mexico, was a capital city of the Maya people between the years 850 and 1221. At its heart is the magnificent Kukulcan pyramid, which has 365 steps – one for each day of the year.

This tornado-shaped part of the planet is a melting pot of nature, people, and cultures old and new. Eight different countries have squished themselves into a twisting bridge of land that joins North and South America. Mexico is by far the biggest – more than twice the size of the others all combined. As you travel south, you'll see the desert-dry dustiness of northern Mexico transforming into lusher, greener, more tropical lands.

History and nature creep in through every sight and sound. The temples and ruins of the Aztec, Maya, Olmec and Toltec peoples, built during the 7th to 15th centuries, peep out from the past, while the surrounding jungle trees try to hide them. Meanwhile, Spanish voices fill the air, the language brought to the Americas by the European conquistadors (conquerors) who arrived in the 16th century.

The curling landmass cradles thousands of Caribbean islands to the east. Sometimes known as the West Indies, these islands are a warm-and-tropical world where violent storms are frequent visitors. This warmth and rain delivers many important foods, too. Much of the world's coffee beans, chocolate, sugar, bananas and citrus fruits sprout up from these lush lands.

Grey whales travel 10,000 kilometres, from the Arctic Circle to the waters off western Mexico, to have their babies.

In Guatemala, the thick rainforest hides Tikal, an ancient city of palaces, markets and towering temple pyramids built by the Maya people.

Scuba divers flock to the Caribbean islands to explore the shipwrecks and coral reefs. Under the surface of the warm sea thousands of colourful fish swim in and out of the forests of precious coral. Turtles and sharks prowl the reefs, too.

You can thank Mexico for chocolate! As early as 900CE, people in this region used the seeds of the cacao tree to prepare a yummy, chocolatey drink, mmmmm.

THE PANAMA CANAL

This human-made marvel is the ultimate shipping shortcut. Since 1914, when the Panama Canal first opened, ships have no longer needed to go all the way around South America to travel to and from the Atlantic and Pacific oceans. This nifty knife of water – almost 80 kilometres long – cuts through one of the slimmest parts of Central America. It's the busiest big-ship canal in the world: between 12,000 and 15,000 vessels drift along it every year.

Yanomami tribe man

The Equator 0°

Chameleon

Timber logging

BRAZIL

• BRASILIA

Toucan

CARIBBEAN SEA

FRENCH GUIANA (FRANCE)
CAYENNE

SURINAME
PARAMARIBO

GUYANA
GEORGETOWN

Amazon River

Amazon Rainforest

Manaus Opera House

Angel Falls

Oil rig

VENEZUELA

• CARACAS

Spider monkey

Quechua woman

Armadillo

BOLIVIA

• LA PAZ

Scarlet macaw

COLOMBIA

• BOGOTA

PERU

• LIMA

• QUITO

ECUADOR

Nazca Lines

Banana tree

Peruvian woman

Llama

SOUTH AMERICA

Janeiro

SOUTH ATLANTIC OCEAN

SOUTH PACIFIC OCEAN

PARAGUAY
• ASUNCION

URUGUAY
• MONTEVIDEO

ARGENTINA
• BUENOS AIRES

CHILE
• SANTIAGO

Black jaguar

Andean mountain range

Sheep

Vineyards

Cattle ranching

Humboldt penguin

Rockhopper penguin

FALKLAND ISLANDS (UK)

→ Stanley

The Beagle

SOUTH GEORGIA & SOUTH SANDWICH ISLANDS

Sardine shoal

Bronze whaler shark

Southern right whale

Mackerel

Fishing boat

Yerba mate tea

Motmot bird

Tropic of Capricorn
23.43718°S

SOUTH AMERICA

In the tropics, it's terrifically warm and rainy all year round. The conditions here make the air very humid, which means it's full of moisture. This is fantastic news for plants and animals, which thrive in these conditions.

South America is like a tall, tropical animal that hangs down from the looping branches of Central America. It's a 'chameleon' continent full of very different environments, from its broad, bushy head down to its chillier, curling tail. A warm-and-steamy rainforest sits in its eastern belly, while a chain of lofty mountains runs up and down its bony western spine.

The Amazon region wraps a third of the continent in tropical rainforest – the biggest in the world. Meanwhile, the Atacama, to the west, is the driest hot desert we have. Up at the Angel Falls, in Venezuela, water tumbles to the ground over a record distance of almost a kilometre.

There are big highs and lows in the southern parts, too: the Andes mountains are almost seven kilometres high in places, while the Pampas grasslands, to the east, are low, vast and flat – where the continent's cowboys, called gauchos, round up their sheep, cattle and horses. The continent's southern tail is just a thousand kilometres from Antarctica. It's so cool that you might spot the 'rockstar' rockhopper penguins there, with their crests that look like punky hair.

Rainforests only cover about six per cent of the planet's surface, yet more than half of all plant and animal species in the world make themselves at home there.

PACKED WITH NATURE

There is more wildlife in the Amazon rainforest than in any other place on the planet. It's home to roughly 430 different kinds of mammals, 1,300 different bird species, 3,000 different kinds of fish, 40,000 types of plants, and - brace yourself - more than 30 MILLION different kinds of insects!

The Amazon, in South America, is by far the largest tropical rainforest on the planet. If we could shift it all to Australia, it would cover about 90 per cent of that entire continent!

THE BIG CITIES

Brazil is South America's biggest country. It covers nearly half of the continent and contains well over 200 million Brazilians. Its largest cities are São Paulo and Rio de Janeiro. In Rio, a big carnival takes place every year. It lasts four days and features millions of people in spectacular costumes - dancing, singing and playing musical instruments.

THE RAINFOREST

The tropical rainforests are a thick, green belt blooming to the north and south of the equator, that invisible line that runs around the earth. Leaping from leaf to leaf, you'll find these beautiful rainforests in Central and South America, West and Central Africa, India, Southeast Asia, New Guinea and northeastern Australia.

LIFE IN LAYERS

Tall trees knit together into an 'emergent' layer, where nimble birds and monkeys can nip about, foraging and feeding. Most rainforest animals live in the layer below this, the 'canopy', where the vegetation is thick, tasty, and good for hiding or making a den. Then there's an 'understory' of smaller trees and shrubs, and the shady 'forest floor' and river banks, beneath.

THE BIG BULLIES

Rainforest predators swoop from up high and prowl down low . . . The harpy eagle can snatch a sloth or a howler monkey from the trees, using its powerful talons. Meanwhile, caimans, jaguars and giant otters patrol the shadowy depths.

EUROPE

Gyrfalcon

Narwhal

Geyser

Icelandic pony

ICELAND

•REYKJAVIK

Soay sheep

Puffin

Storm petrel

ST KILDA

Stone cleit

Balmoral Castle

Giant's Causeway

Shamrock

Bluefin tuna

Book of Kells

Swordfish

ATLANTIC OCEAN

CANARY ISLANDS (SPAIN)

LANZAROTE

TENERIFE

LA GOMERA

Squid

Fair Isle jumper

Oystercatcher

Lewis chessmen

Orkney chair

Pictish cross

Loch Ness Monster

Edinburgh

Highland cow

UNITED KINGDOM

Belfast•

Forth Bridge

DUBLIN•

IRELAND

Cardiff•

LONDON •

NORTH SEA

FAIR ISLE

Leif Erikson's route

Leif Erikson

Viking ship

NORWAY

OSLO•

DENMARK

COPENHAGEN•

Tromso Cathedral

Pine marten

SWEDEN

STOCKHOL

Little Merm

AMSTERDAM•

NETHERLANDS

BELGIUM•

BRUSSELS

LUXEMBOURG

LUXEMBOURG

Eiffel Tower

•PARIS

FRANCE

Frankfurt

BERLIN•

GERMANY

LIECHTENSTEIN

VADUZ•

BERN•

SWITZERLAND

Rialto Bridge

MONACO

ANDORRA

PORTUGAL

MADRID•

LISBON

SPAIN

Dama de Elche statue

Mediterranean Sea

Colosseum

ROME•

Tower of Pisa

PRAGUE•

CZECH REPUBLI

VIENNA•

•BRAT

AUSTRIA

HUN

SLOVENIA

LJUBLJANA•

ZAGREB•

CROATIA

SAN MARINO

BOSNIA & HERZEGOVI

ITALY

MONTENEG

PODGORICA

TIRA

Mount Etna

VALLETTA•

MALTA

30

Dried fish

Reindeer herder

Barn swallow

FINLAND

St Petersburg

ESTONIA

LATVIA

ANIA

US•

•MINSK

BELARUS

Stork

•KIEV

UKRAINE

European bison

Ukrainian woman

MOLDOVA

•CHISINAU

MANIA

ESTI•

GARIA

Moldovan church

BLACK SEA

Pelican

TURKEY

Romany women

Houses of Santorini

Olive branch

•NICOSIA

CYPRUS

BARENTS SEA

Seal

WHITE SEA

Mute swan

RUSSIA

Bear

Ural Mountains

Mari woman

St. Basil's Cathedral

MOSCOW•

Russian girl

Grey wolf

Carpathian shepherd

Romanian shepherd

Romany caravan

EUROPE

Europe stretches from the Scandinavian countries shivering inside the Arctic Circle to the islands sunbathing in the Mediterranean Sea, and from ocean-facing Portugal in the west to Russia's Ural Mountains in the east.

In the north, the Scandinavian countries hang down from the Arctic like icicles. To the west, the British Isles are a collection of countries in the Atlantic Ocean, lush lands of history and heritage. Back across the sea you'll find the Low Countries are just that – low and as flat as pancakes.

Travelling across central Europe takes you from France – a land of high-speed trains zooming through farms, fields and vineyards and cities – through Germany, criss-crossed and cut up by rivers. Then you'll climb into the Alpine region, the tallest, snow-capped heights of Central Europe.

Moving east, lie the Baltic countries of Estonia, Latvia, Lithuania, Belarus, Moldova and Ukraine. Eastern Europe is a place of wildlife, too: grey wolves patrol the Carpathian Mountains, while wild bison roam the snowy forests of Poland. Many eastern cities are rich in reminders of different times and cultures. Prague, in the Czech Republic, has buildings from eight different centuries.

In the south, in Portugal and Spain, the summer weather is hot, the fiestas (festivals) are colourful and the food is delicious. Italy is the leg-shaped limb of Europe, while Greece is a place where ancient and modern ways of life meet and mix: fishing boats drift along routes once crossed by ancient traders, while farmers still produce things they traded thousands of years ago – wheat, olives, figs, grapes, cheese, honey, wine and citrus fruits.

The Basque Country is a region of northern Spain, where the people share a unique culture and speak Basque or Euskara, one of the oldest languages in Europe.

KEEPING THE DUTCH DRY

Around a third of The Netherlands (also known as Holland) is below sea level! The Dutch have used sand dunes, dams, floodgates and special earth banks called dykes to prevent water from surging onto the land during sea storms. A system of electric pumping stations and canals also helps to keep the land nicely drained.

Brussels, in Belgium, can boast of being the 'capital of Europe'. This is where the Parliament of the European Union is based.

AN ANCIENT CITY

The Parthenon, in Athens, is a temple that was dedicated to Athena, goddess of many things including wisdom, courage, civilization and Athens itself. It was built in the 5th century BCE.

Fruit crumble (UK)

Roast beef (UK)

MOU-TARD

Bag
(Fr

Olives and banderillas (Spain)

Croissant (France)

Sunday roast (UK)

Sausage and gherkin (Germany)

Pizza (Italy)

Fish and chips (UK)

Greek salad (Greece)

Padrón peppers (Spain)

Salmon, red cabbage and potato (Sweden)

Mussels and frites (Belgium)

Souvlaki (Greece)

Meatballs (Denmark, Sweden)

Gelato (Italy)

Borscht Soup (Russia)

Haggis (Scotland)

Cassoulet (France)

Pumpernickel bread (Eastern Europe)

BUTTER

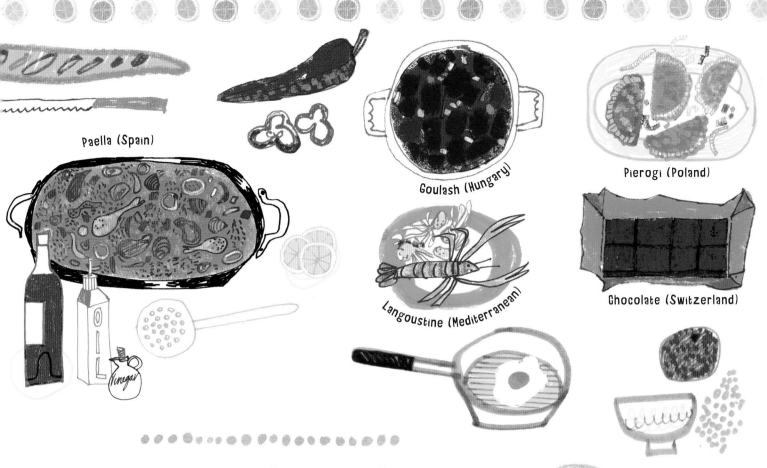

Paella (Spain)

Goulash (Hungary)

Pierogi (Poland)

Langoustine (Mediterranean)

Chocolate (Switzerland)

Eat your way round Europe with Swedish meatballs, a British roast dinner, a French baguette, Spanish olives, Belgian mussels and chips, German sausage, a buttery French croissant, Swiss chocolate, Polish pierogi, Hungarian goulash, Greek salad . . . Full yet?!

Waffle (Belgium)

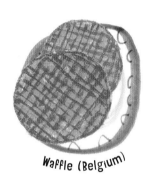

Sachertorte (Austria)

EUROPEAN

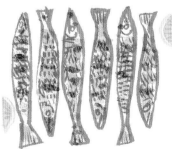

Sardines (Portugal)

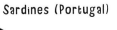

FOOD!

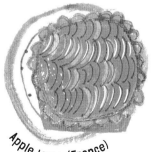

Apple tarte (France)

Grapes (Italy)

AFRICA

Koutoubia mosque

MOROCCO
●RABAT

ALGERIA
●ALGIERS

TUNISIA
●TUNIS

Tuareg People

TRIPOLI●

Oasis

Lepis Magna

LIBYA

CAIRO●
Pyramids

EGYPT

Camel traders

SUDAN

●KHARTOUM

ERITREA
●ASMARA

DJIBOUTI
DJIBOUTI●

ETHIOPIA
ADDIS ABABA●

SOMALIA

Gazelle

MOGADISHU●

Felucca boat

The Equator 0°

Acacia/Flame tree

KENYA
●NAIROBI

Lion

SOUTH SUDAN
●JUBA

UGANDA
●KAMPALA

RWANDA---●KIGALI
BURUNDI
●BUJUMBURA

DEMO
REPUBLI

Gorilla

Horned desert viper

NIGER
●NIAMEY

CHAD
●N'DJAMENA

CENTRAL AFRICAN REPUBLIC
●BANGUI

Musgum huts

CAMEROON
●YAOUNDÉ

REPUBLIC
OF CONGO
BRAZZAVILLE●

GABON
LIBREVILLE●

KINSHASA

Stork

WESTERN SAHARA
LAAYOUNE●

MAURITANIA
●NOUAKCHOTT

Dogon houses

MALI

SENEGAL
DAKAR●

THE GAMBIA
BANJUL●

BISSAU●
GUINEA-BISSAU

GUINEA
CONAKRY●

SIERRA LEONE
FREETOWN●

Diamonds

LIBERIA
MONROVIA●

IVORY COAST
YAMOUSSOUKRO●

BURKINA FASO
OUAGADOUGOU●

BAMAKO●

GHANA
ACCRA●

TOGO
LOMÉ●

BENIN
PORTO NOVO●

NIGERIA
●ABUJA

Well

GULF OF GUINEA

EQUATORIAL GUINEA
MALABO●

SÃO TOMÉ●
SÃO TOMÉ & PRINCIPE

Nigerian men

AFRICA

Africa spreads out over the Equator like a stretching lion. It is the only continent to stretch all the way from the northern to southern temperate zones.

Covering more than half of northern Africa, the Sahara is the biggest hot desert in the world. Northwest of this giant sandpit are the lofty Atlas Mountains. To the east, in Egypt, there's a rich, fertile valley around the River Nile. The Blue and White Nile combine to form the longest stretch of river in the world. South of the great desert, you'll find a tropical band around the belly of the continent, where coffee beans, cocoa beans, cassava roots, bananas, yams, wheat, peanuts and cotton grow. Oil and minerals bring wealth to the states around the Gulf of Guinea.

The heart of central Africa beats with the sounds of tropical rainforests. The shrieks of chimpanzees, chatter of gorillas and squawks of the jungle birds fill the air. Lush, tangled jungle stretches east towards the Great Rift Valley. Here, the land dips and dives into huge, deep lakes and swells into volcanoes and mountains - the biggest of all, Mount Kilimanjaro, soaring 5,895 metres into the sky.

ANCIENT EGYPT

Ancient Egypt was one of the world's most successful civilizations. The River Nile was its lifeline. Each summer, heavy rains caused the river to flood the land, leaving it full of nutrients - perfect for growing crops. Farmers dug waterways to store some of the floodwaters, so that they could water their crops when the weather was dry.

The pyramids at Giza, Egypt, were built as tombs for three pharaohs (kings) named Khufu, Khafre and Menkaure. The oldest one was built more than 4,500 years ago.

NOMADS

The Tuareg people of the Sahara are nomads. They make their living by keeping on the move. They shift their camels, sheep and goats around the desert in search of water and places for the animals to graze. The Tuareg call themselves the Imohag, which means 'free people'.

Dust storms can sweep grains of sand from the Sahara to lands thousands of kilometres away!

An oasis is a place in the desert where water sloshes up from underground, so that plants can grow.

Desert reptiles - such as the horned desert viper - slink around, searching for snacks.

The Maasai people live in tribal communities along the Great Rift Valley, in southern Kenya and northern Tanzania.

MYSTERIOUS GORILLAS

Western lowland gorillas live in the rainforests of central and western Africa. They live in areas so deep and remote that even animal experts don't know how many gorillas survive there.

AFRICAN GRASSLANDS

On the valley floors, in between the peaks and troughs, the land reaches out into the broad, flat savannah. This gargantuan grassland region is not just a gigantic lawn of wild plants and grasses – it is a complicated universe of life.

The savannah is home to huge herds of zebras, wildebeest and antelopes, with giraffes, rhinos, elephants and aardvarks among those roaming alongside them. These creatures are kept on their toes by the lions, cheetahs and other predators who are constantly on the hunt for prey.

WATERING HOLES

Lots of different animals meet at watering holes to drink, swim and wash. But they have to be careful in the dry season . . .
As the watering holes dry up and get smaller, animals need to paddle in further to get a sip of water. A crafty crocodile might be waiting in the middle to pounce.

HERE COMES THE RAIN!

The hot summer brings a rainy season, from May to November. Suddenly, grasses, thorn bushes and an explosion of other plants and flowers burst into life.

SAVANNAH SUPERSTAR

The cheetah is one of nature's great record-breakers. When sprinting over short distances, the animal can reach speeds of up to 120km/h.

WEST ASIA

Pasqueflower

Owl

Jade

Wild boar

MONGOLIA

Tibetan nomad

RUSSIA

Baikonur rocket

Hoopoe bird

Shale/Oil

Russian bearskin hat

Ural Mountain house

KAZAKHSTAN

ASTANA

BARENTS SEA

woman tribeswoman

Turkmenistan elder

St Petersburg

MOSCOW

Russian babushka

UZBEKISTAN

NORWEGIAN SEA

EUROPE

Sufi whirling dancers

CASPIAN SEA

GEORGIA

TBILISI

AZERBAIJAN

Reindeer

Orange

Pomegranate

BLACK SEA

TURKEY

ANKARA

Istanbul

YEREVAN

Grapes

Panda

TAJIKISTAN

AFGHANISTAN
Hissar Fortress
KABUL
ISLAMABAD
Afghan tribal nomad

•TEHRAN

Bam Citadel
Manul cat

KUWAIT
KUWAIT CITY
BAHRAIN
MANAMA
•BAGHDAD
Oil field

JORDAN
•AMMAN
Al Malwiya Mosque
Great Mosque Mecca
Red Sea coral
Equator
Figs

SAUDI ARABIA
•RIYADH
Bronze head. Sargon the Great
Saudi Arabian women
Hawk

Date palm

QATAR
•DOHA
•DUBAI
U.A.E.
Oil well

OMAN
MUSCAT•

Dragon's blood tree

YEMEN
•SANA'A
Yemeni village
Arabian oryx

GULF OF OMAN
Leopard gecko

ARABIAN SEA

INDIAN OCEAN

Mount
EVEREST
8848M

PAKISTAN
Tomb of Bibi Jawindi

Rice plant
BHUTAN
THIMPHU•
BANGLADESH
DHAKA•

NEW DELHI
INDIA

NEPAL
KATHMANDU•
Yak

Mangoes

MYANMAR
NAYPYIDAW•

Stilt house

BAY OF BENGAL

Bengal tiger

Ganges River dolphin

Taj Mahal

Mumbai•

Cinnamon
Chai tea

SRI LANKA
•COLOMBO
Sloth bear

Tea picker

Malavath Poorna

Phanthog

Oxygen system

Jute rope

Altimeter

Jordan Romero

Sherpa Tenzing Norgay

Junko Tabei

Sir Edmund Hillary

Tropic of Capricorn
23:43'18"S

EAST ASIA

PACIFIC OCEAN

Cherry blossom

Herring

Shimofuri goby

Japanese macaque

Tokyo Skytree

JAPAN

TOKYO•

SEA OF JAPAN

Ropits Robot car

NORTH KOREA

SEOUL•

SOUTH KOREA

Weather dish

Iceberg

Polar bear

Udege man

Weather/Research post

Woolly mammoth

Nenet woman

Siberian tiger

Nong'an Pagoda

PYONGYANG•

Songyue Pagoda

BEIJING•

Terracotta

EAST SIBERIAN SEA

Siberian house

Walrus

Trans-Siberian Railway

RUSSIA

Irkutsk Tower

Lake Baikal seal

Yurt

ULAANBAATAR•

MONGOLIA

Mongolian horse

Great Wall of China

Orcas

Fisherman

Russian hat

Cashmere goat

Mongolian Man

Silk cocoons

Mackerel

Grouper fish

PHILIPPINE SEA

Proboscis monkey

Tarsier

Chinese junk boat

Palm tree

Sun bear

TIMOR-LESTE

DILI

Rice paddy house

Chiang Kai-Shek Memorial Hall

PHILIPPINES

TAIPEI

TAIWAN

Tram

MANILA

INDONESIA

Dim sum

Jeepney

BANDAR SERI BEGAWAN

MALAYSIA

Baby Borneo Pygmy elephant

Guilin fisherman

Hong Kong

SOUTH CHINA SEA

Baby orangutan

BRUNEI

Hot pot

VIETNAM

SINGAPORE

JAKARTA

Water buffalo

HANOI

Supertree buildings (Singapore)

Nutmeg

LAOS

CAMBODIA

KUALA LUMPUR

Mace

VIENTIANE

THAILAND

PHNOM PENH

Minangkabau house

Carrying rice

MYANMAR

BANGKOK

NAYPYIDAW

Panda

BHUTAN

THIMPHU

BANGLADESH

ANDAMAN & NICOBAR ISLANDS

Indonesian Muslim woman

Buddhist monk

DHAKA

NEPAL

INDIA

BAY OF BENGAL

INDIAN OCEAN

KATHMANDU

Clouded leopard

Padaung woman

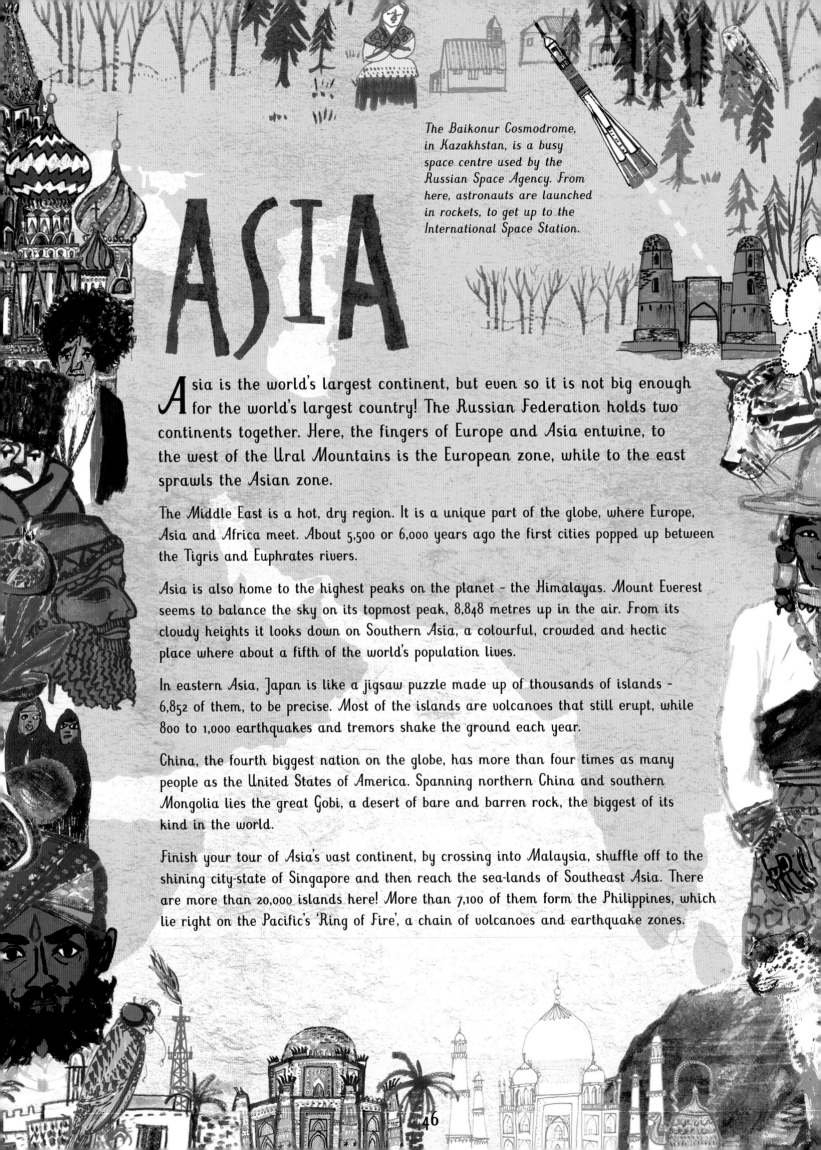

ASIA

The Baikonur Cosmodrome, in Kazakhstan, is a busy space centre used by the Russian Space Agency. From here, astronauts are launched in rockets, to get up to the International Space Station.

Asia is the world's largest continent, but even so it is not big enough for the world's largest country! The Russian Federation holds two continents together. Here, the fingers of Europe and Asia entwine, to the west of the Ural Mountains is the European zone, while to the east sprawls the Asian zone.

The Middle East is a hot, dry region. It is a unique part of the globe, where Europe, Asia and Africa meet. About 5,500 or 6,000 years ago the first cities popped up between the Tigris and Euphrates rivers.

Asia is also home to the highest peaks on the planet – the Himalayas. Mount Everest seems to balance the sky on its topmost peak, 8,848 metres up in the air. From its cloudy heights it looks down on Southern Asia, a colourful, crowded and hectic place where about a fifth of the world's population lives.

In eastern Asia, Japan is like a jigsaw puzzle made up of thousands of islands – 6,852 of them, to be precise. Most of the islands are volcanoes that still erupt, while 800 to 1,000 earthquakes and tremors shake the ground each year.

China, the fourth biggest nation on the globe, has more than four times as many people as the United States of America. Spanning northern China and southern Mongolia lies the great Gobi, a desert of bare and barren rock, the biggest of its kind in the world.

Finish your tour of Asia's vast continent, by crossing into Malaysia, shuffle off to the shining city-state of Singapore and then reach the sea-lands of Southeast Asia. There are more than 20,000 islands here! More than 7,100 of them form the Philippines, which lie right on the Pacific's 'Ring of Fire', a chain of volcanoes and earthquake zones.

THE ENDLESS RAILS

The train ride from Moscow to Vladivostok, in the far east of Russia, is the longest in the world. The Trans-Siberian Railway crosses almost 9,300 kilometres. The trip takes eight days!

The Nenet people live in villages of tents in the pine forests of Siberia. Each year, they travel with gigantic herds of reindeer from their summer feeding grounds in the north to their winter pastures to the south.

In springtime, the Japanese sakura (cherry blossom) trees burst into bloom, carpeting the country in shades of pale pink.

Borneo is the third-largest island on Earth. It's shared between three different nations - Malaysia, Indonesia and Brunei. Orangutans live on the islands of Borneo and Sumatra. Its name means 'person of the forest'.

HIMALAYAS

These mountains were once covered by the ocean, but then - about 40 million years ago - the rocky plates of India and Eurasia (in the Earth's crust) started pushing against each other under the sea floor. This created a huge crumple of rocks, which is now the planet's biggest mountain range. There are fossils of prehistoric sea creatures on Mount Everest - proof that it once stood underwater!

THE INDIAN OCEAN

The Indian Ocean is the Earth's third biggest ocean. It is a warm and wonderful world, which beams brightly with pride. Tropical islands, big and small, are scattered across the ocean's vast shades of blue and green. Lots of islands means lots of coastlines and beaches - and plenty of clear, warm, shallow waters where sun-soaked coral reefs can flourish.

Sea mammals and reptiles come here for the warmth and food. Tropical fish, crustaceans and spineless invertebrates love it, too: spiny lobsters crouch among the reefs, lionfish and spiny devilfish - armed with poisons - find their own hiding places, while the clever mimic octopus copies the colours of other animals (to avoid becoming a meal).

Container ship

ARABIAN SEA

The São Gabriel

MAL

Malindi
Mombasa

Pemba Island

Manta ray

Zanzibar Town
ZANZIBAR

Gentle Giants

From wing to wing, manta rays can be up to seven metres wide. Don't let their monstrous size fool you - they are gentle, docile, and enjoy being stroked by scuba divers!

INDIA

Vasco da Gama's voyage

ANTANANARIVO

MADAGASCAR   MAURITIUS →

← REUNION

Vasco da Gama

Giant tube worm

Spiny lobster

Hydrothermal vent

HYDROTHERMAL VENTS

More than two kilometres below sea level, on the seabed, hydrothermal vents spout super-hot water and minerals. This cocktail of goodness feeds a gang of sun-shy creatures, from giant tube worms to vent clams, eelpout fish and squat lobsters.

Mimic octopus

BAY OF BENGAL

ANDAMAN SEA

SOUTH CHINA SEA

GULF OF THAILAND

alicut
ozhikode)

Warm Waters

Humpback whales always feed in cooler waters and then head to warmer places to have their babies. They often give birth to their little ones in the warm waters south of India.

back whale

Tropicbird

Equator

JAVA SEA

ack whale calf

Hammerhead shark

CEAN

CHRISTMAS ISLAND

FLYING FISH COVE

MURRAY HILL

fety in Numbers

antic shoals (groups) of sardines
d mackerels keep together, wary
bigger predators.

Whale shark

Lionfish

The blue whale is the biggest beast on the planet!

ue whale

Coelacanth

Rock art crocodile

SOUTH CHINA SEA

PHILIPPINES

Great white shark

NORTHERN MARIANA ISLANDS (USA)

Rock art fish

MARSHALL ISLANDS

PALAU

Barracuda

MICRONESIA

Blue-ringed octopus

Saltwater crocodile

Dugong

INDONESIA

PAPUA NEW GUINEA

PORT MORESBY ★

NAURU

Fish sculpture

SOLOMON ISLANDS

Stilt house

TIMOR SEA

Pearl fishing

Prawn boat

Darwin

NORTHERN TERRITORY

Wallaby

Torres Straits Islander woman

Torres Straits Islander elder

VANUATU

CORAL SEA

Kangaroo

Rock art emu

NEW CALEDONIA (FRANCE)

Uluru

Thorny devil lizard

WESTERN AUSTRALIA

Road train

AUSTRALIA

SOUTH AUSTRALIA

QUEENSLAND

Brisbane

Platypus

Sydney Harbour Bridge

Blue tongued lizard

The Pinnacles

Perth

Wheatbelt

Sheep

Mining truck

NEW SOUTH WALES

Sydney

Sydney Opera House

Boom

Black swan

Grapes

GREAT AUSTRALIAN BIGHT

Adelaide

CANBERRA

VICTORIA

TASMAN SEA

Fairy penguin

Melbourne

Kiwi

Great white shark

Aboriginal man

Echidna

Kookaburra

Kimberley rock art

TASMANIA

Koala

HOBART

Tasmanian Devil

Oil rig

Albatross

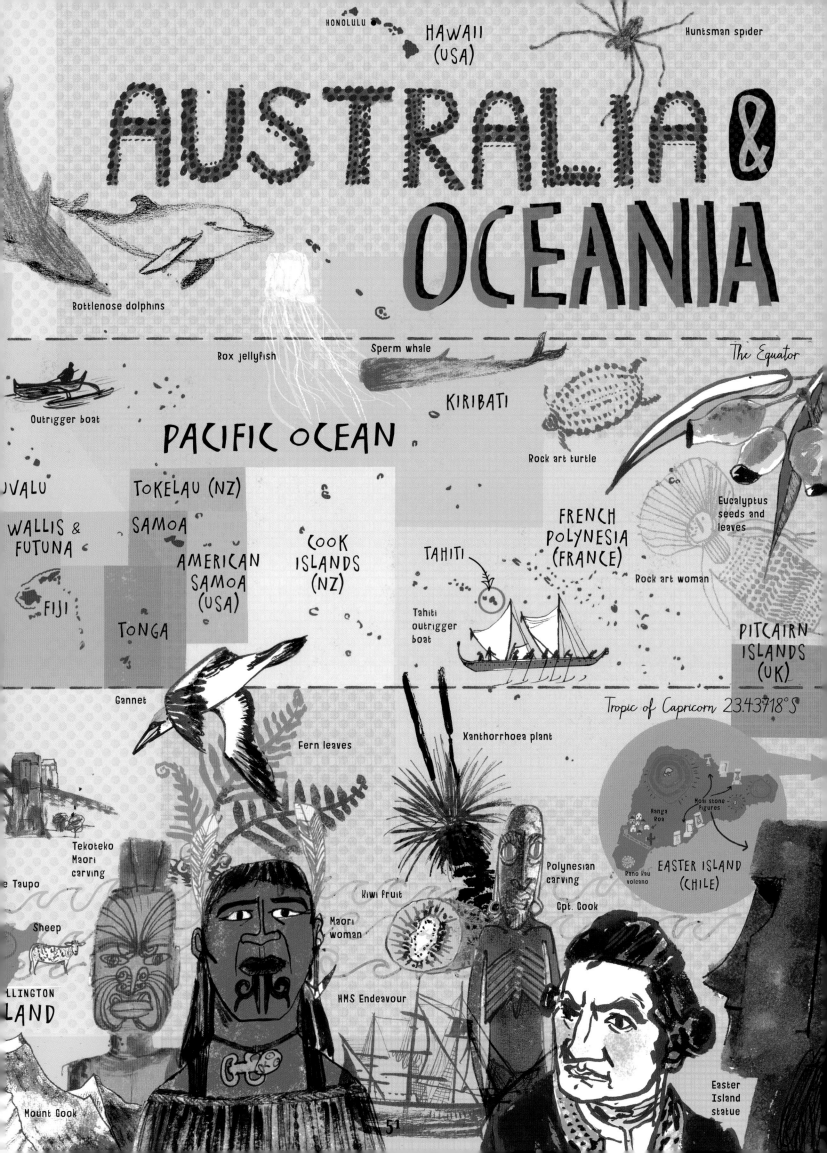

HONOLULU

HAWAII (USA)

Huntsman spider

AUSTRALIA & OCEANIA

Bottlenose dolphins

Box jellyfish

Sperm whale

The Equator

Outrigger boat

KIRIBATI

PACIFIC OCEAN

Rock art turtle

Eucalyptus seeds and leaves

UVALU

TOKELAU (NZ)

WALLIS & FUTUNA

SAMOA

FRENCH POLYNESIA (FRANCE)

COOK ISLANDS (NZ)

Rock art woman

AMERICAN SAMOA (USA)

TAHITI

FIJI

TONGA

Tahiti outrigger boat

PITCAIRN ISLANDS (UK)

Gannet

Tropic of Capricorn 23.43718°S

Fern leaves

Xanthorrhoea plant

Hanga Roa

Moai stone figures

Tekoteko Maori carving

Polynesian carving

e Taupo

Kiwi fruit

Rano Kau volcano

EASTER ISLAND (CHILE)

Sheep

Maori woman

Cpt. Cook

LLINGTON LAND

HMS Endeavour

Mount Cook

Easter Island statue

AUSTRALIA & OCEANIA

Australia is a gigantic slab of land, covering more than seven-and-a-half million square kilometres. Most of the world's continents connect with at least one other, but Australia is an island and a continent all of its own.

Australia is famous for its outback. These wild, untamed parts of the country stretch right across the middle, with deserts dominating the western half. The climate is cooler and wetter around the edges of the landmass, where all the biggest cities can be found. In the northeast, there are thick patches of tropical rainforest.

New Zealand's two main islands are known for having up to 20 times more sheep than people! The North Island has active volcanoes and the super-large Lake Taupo, which lies inside a crater formed by an exploding volcano. South Island's backbone is the Southern Alps, and it has a chilly coastline of forests and glaciers.

Oceania is the part of the planet where water takes over from land. Thousands of islands spray out in different directions like droplets splashing into the vast Pacific Ocean. Many of these islands are the rocky tips of underwater volcanoes and mountain ranges. Around 2,500 years ago, the Polynesians were masters of the seas of this region. To carry their people and animals from island to island, they built canoes out of tree trunks, palm leaves and ropes woven from coconut fibres.

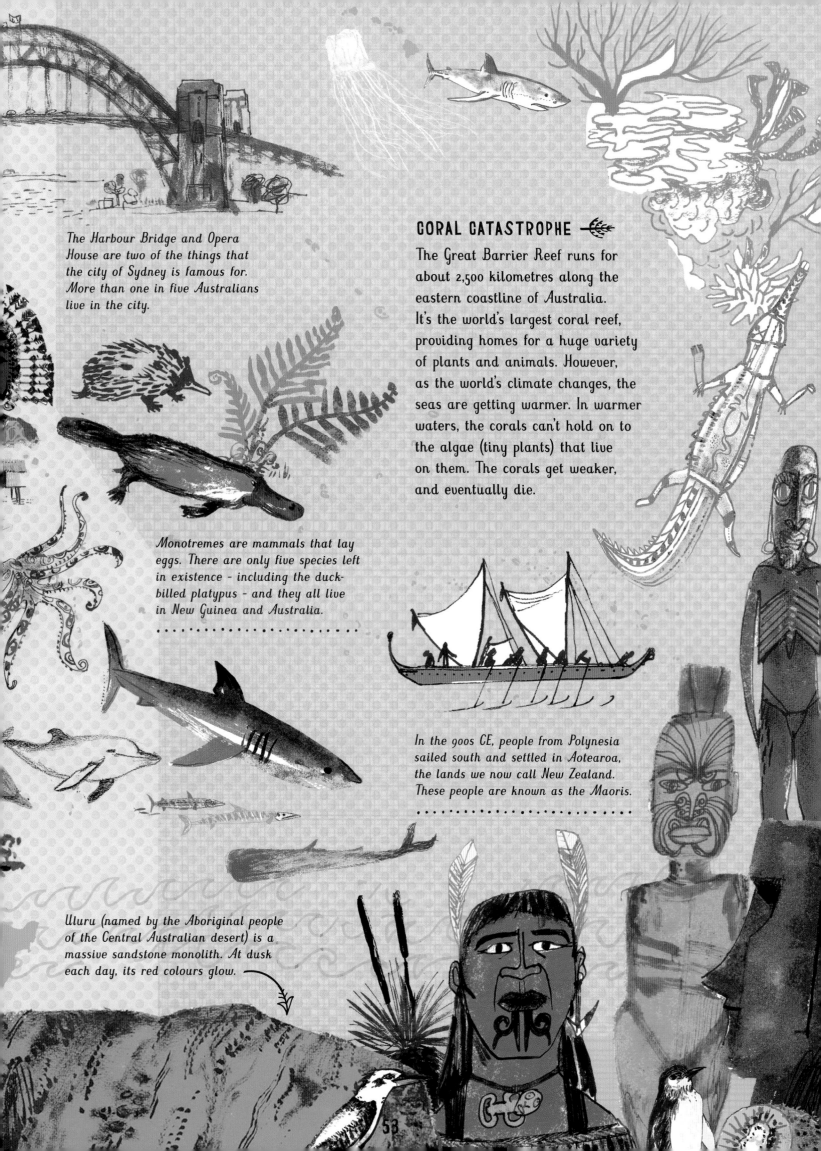

The Harbour Bridge and Opera House are two of the things that the city of Sydney is famous for. More than one in five Australians live in the city.

CORAL CATASTROPHE

The Great Barrier Reef runs for about 2,500 kilometres along the eastern coastline of Australia. It's the world's largest coral reef, providing homes for a huge variety of plants and animals. However, as the world's climate changes, the seas are getting warmer. In warmer waters, the corals can't hold on to the algae (tiny plants) that live on them. The corals get weaker, and eventually die.

Monotremes are mammals that lay eggs. There are only five species left in existence - including the duck-billed platypus - and they all live in New Guinea and Australia.

In the 900s CE, people from Polynesia sailed south and settled in Aotearoa, the lands we now call New Zealand. These people are known as the Maoris.

Uluru (named by the Aboriginal people of the Central Australian desert) is a massive sandstone monolith. At dusk each day, its red colours glow.

AUSTRALIAN ·OUTBACK·

BY GUM

The eucalyptus, or gum tree, is an important Australian plant. Its leaves give off oil that is used as a medicine to help breathing, and as a poison to kill insects. The blue haze of the oil misting up from eucalyptus forests gives the Blue Mountains near Sydney their name. This tough tree can survive fire, and endures drought by dropping leaves and twigs so they don't lose water. It is the only food that koalas can eat.

DANGER?

Australia has a reputation for being home to dangerous wildlife! Venomous spiders, snakes, jellyfish, powerful crocodiles and ferocious sharks are creatures that can kill - but these magnificent animals are more at risk from humans than we are from them.

A WILD CONTINENT APART

Millions of years ago, the continent of Australia was the first to drift away from the others. Separated from the rest of the world, its wildlife developed quite differently from everywhere else, and today it is home to animals unlike any others on the planet. A huge proportion of its animal species are found only in Australia.

BRILLIANT BIRDS

The emu is the world's second-largest bird, and like the largest, the ostrich, it cannot fly. Other well-known Australian birds include cockatoos, kookaburras and Australia's own penguin, the little penguin (or fairy penguin).

ATLANTIC OCEAN

Wandering albatross

SOUTH GEORGIA &
SOUTH SANDWICH ISLANDS

Blackfin icefish

King penguins

Humpback whale

SOUTH AMERICA

Antarctic tern

WEDDE
SEA

Orca spyhop

Adelie penguin

Cape petrel

PACIFIC
OCEAN

Research ship

Antarctic tern

Vinson
4892

Icebergs

Krill

1911 Expedition

Eelpout fish

Blue whale

AMUNDSEN SEA

Sea kelp

Fin whale

Humpback whale

Minke whale

Scott of
the Antarctic

Ernest
Shackleton

1911 Expedition
dog, Chris

Scott's diary

Captain
Robert
Scott
Diary
1911

Apsley
Cherry-
Garrard

ANTARCTICA

Hourglass dolphin

Snow petrel

Dog sled team. Byrd Expedition 1928–30

Cyclist – Snow bike

INDIAN OCEAN

Tourists

Weddell seal

Halley base (UK)

MAWSON

Mawson base (Aus)

Hagglund vehicle

Penguins

Leopard seal

SOUTHERN OCEAN

Helen Skelton

Amundsen–Scott base (USA)

Emperor penguin

Man–hauler

90° East

South Pole

Mt. Erebus 3794m

Mt. Terror 3230m

Emperor penguin egg

International scientists

ROSS SEA

180° North

Dr Mary Alice McWhinnie

Roald Amundsen

Maria V. Klenova

Ann Daniels

ANTARCTICA

The isolated, southern continent of Antarctica is by far the driest place on the planet, a frosty, glacial, ice-capped desert. It gets a tiny sprinkling of about 200 millilitres of snow each year along the coasts, and even less at its inland areas.

Antarctica is the polar world on the bottom of the globe, enveloping roughly 13.75 million kilometres of land in ice. It's one of the smaller continents - bigger than Europe and Australia, but smaller than South America. An enormous cap of ice covers 98 per cent of the continent - enough to cover the whole of Europe. Around Antarctica's edges, huge chunks of ice snap off and become icebergs.

Despite the cold, it's one of the world's wildlife hotspots. Adélie, emperor, chinstrap and gentoo penguins hop on and off the ice, hoping to bag a belly-full of fish, squid and krill before an orca or leopard seal attacks. It's a wide world of whales, too, with humpbacks blowing bubble nets to trap small fish and krill, while others skim the surface or swell their throats with water to find their fill of food.

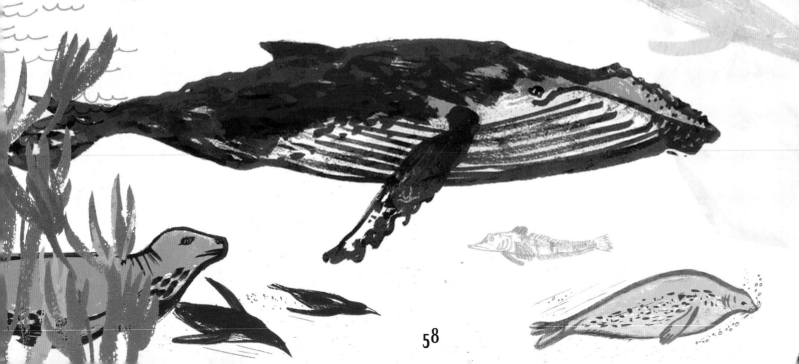

The Southern Lights (or Aurora Australis) are a natural display of colours in the sky, created by charged particles colliding with the Earth's atmosphere.

At any one time, between 50 and 200 people live and work at the Amundsen-Scott South Pole Station.

RACE TO THE SOUTH POLE!

In 1091, Robert Falcon Scott and Ernest Shackleton led a British team of explorers trying to reach the South Pole. They had to turn back after two months. In 1907-1909, Shackleton made another attempt and got within 156 kilometres of the South Pole, but was forced to retreat when supplies ran out.

In 1910-11, the race to the South Pole was still on, and there was a head-to-head race to be the first to reach it. Robert Falcon Scott's team was up against Roald Amundsen and his Norwegian crew. Amundsen's team sailed to an Antarctic bay that gave them a big advantage over the British team, and went on to reach the South Pole on 14 December, 1911. Thirty three days later Scott and his crew did the same. Sadly, Scott and many of his crew died on the return journey. Apsley Cherry-Garrard was one who survived, and went on to write a book called 'The Worst Journey in the World'.

LIFE IN ANTARCTICA

Antarctica is the coldest place on the planet, with icy winds, hardly any rain or snow, and dark, dark winters. It's an incredibly inhospitable world . . . but somehow, many different animals make it their home. You won't find any snakes or lizards though – Antarctica is the only continent without reptiles.

FROM MICROSCOPIC TO MEGA-SIZED

Krill are the tiny, shrimp-like creatures that are food for many animals in the Southern Ocean. At some times of the year there are several million tonnes of krill drifting around in enormous swarms in the water. At the other end of the size spectrum are some much bigger animals. The blue whale, despite its size, feeds on krill – devouring up to 3,500 kilograms per day and the southern elephant seals weigh an incredible 4,000 kilograms!

A CHILLY PLACE TO DO SCIENCE

There are no countries or towns in Antarctica, but people do live there for short periods of time. There are research stations all over the continent, where scientists study the climate, environment and wildlife.

PREDATORS ON ICE

It's a tough life in the Antarctic, and predators have to be super-powerful to survive. If an orca (or killer whale) gets impatient while waiting for seals or penguins to enter the water, it might just grab one off an ice shelf instead. The leopard seal has super-sharp, powerful jaws designed to sink into shellfish, seabirds, squids, fish and penguins.

HOW TO KEEP AN EGG WARM

When a female emperor penguin has laid an egg, the male snuggles it into a warm space between his feet, where there's a soft, feathery pocket of skin. This keeps the egg cosy until it hatches – even in temperatures as low as -60°C.

Icefish have an anti-freeze substance in their blood, to stop it from freezing solid.

Glossary

atmosphere Gases surrounding our planet

climate Weather conditions

continents Seven huge zones that the Earth is divided into

cubic metre Volume of a cube with edges that are one metre long

diverse Different

dynamic Exciting and full of new things

forage Search for food

humid Lots of moisture in the air

hydrothermal Hot water in the Earth's crust

marsupial Mammal that carries its babies in a pouch

migrating Animals moving from one area to another

monotreme Mammal that lays eggs

nomads People who travel around to different places rather than having one home

orbit Path of an object travelling around a planet or a star

particles Tiny pieces

pastures Land covered with grass and other plants that animals can eat

pharaoh Ancient Egyptian king

pilgrimage Journey made to a holy place

predator Animal that hunts and eats other animals

prehistoric Time before written records of history began

polar The North or South pole (opposite ends of the Earth)

reefs Ridges of coral below the surface of the sea

savannah Grassland

temperate zones Areas of the Earth that never get extremely hot or cold

tornado Huge spinning wind storm that looks like a long, funnel-shaped cloud

trenches Long, narrow ditches in the ocean bed

tundra Frozen plains of the Arctic regions

twister Another name for a tornado

Index